In Search of Great

by John Nolan

U.S. Copyright TXu 883-089 November 19, 1998
First Edition 2001
Second Edition 2012

This book is dedicated to Lily Roche, Ed O'Keefe and my father, Bill Nolan, and to all those who helped light the way in my search for the truth. I have credited them all in the body of this work, rather than bury their names on some acknowledgements page that no one would read.

Chapter One: Unanswered Questions

I never met my great-uncle Patrick O'Keefe of Waterford, Ireland. He died long before I was born. There are so many questions I'd like to ask him. As a third-class male passenger who survived the sinking of the "unsinkable" *Titanic*, Pat was indeed a rare man. Nearly five hundred men sailed third class on *Titanic*. Only 69 survived, according to the final report issued by the U.S. Senate Subcommittee of the Committee on Commerce in the 1912 investigation. Pat O'Keefe settled in New York City after the tragedy, and eventually joined my family by marrying Anna Nolan, the sister of my grandfather, John "Jack" Nolan, whom I am named after. Pat and Anna O'Keefe had two children, Margaret and Edward. Margaret never married and died in 1988. Edward O'Keefe was still alive, but no one in my family could tell me where he lives. I was told he married and had children. ("A couple of girls," according to Uncle Eddie Nolan.) Thinking that his girls have married and changed their names, I realized that Edward may be the last to carry his family name in America. I had to find Ed O'Keefe!

Most Americans associate April 15th with the income tax filing deadline, but it is also the anniversary of the most famous maritime disaster in history. The great ship went down at approximately 2:20 a.m.(ship's time) on Monday, April 15th, 1912 after hitting an iceberg about 400 miles off the coast of Newfoundland. Over 1,500 lives were lost. Excessive speed and failure to heed ice warnings were among the reasons for the collision. The reasons for the magnitude of the disaster are more complicated.

Long after the release of James Cameron's blockbuster *Titanic* movie, "Titanic-mania" shows no sign of letting up. Even before the film premiered Christmas of 1997, I decided to find out what I could about Great Uncle Pat. I first got hooked on *Titanic* when I saw the 1958 English film, "A Night To Remember," based on Walter Lord's book. Of course I didn't see it back in 1958. I was only three years old then. I saw the film on television many times while growing up. It is considered by many to be the finest *Titanic* movie. Kenneth More's performance as Second Officer Charles Lightoller was captivating, but it was James Cameron's movie that caused an explosion of interest in the *Titanic* story. The Cameron film was such a huge success I found myself swept along in this new wave of fascination, all the while trying to temper my enthusiasm by remembering what a great tragedy it was. Babies froze to death in their mothers' arms in the middle of the icy North Atlantic in pitch black darkness. Wives and children who were fortunate enough to be in a lifeboat watched in horror as husbands and fathers went down with the ship to endure great suffering and death. Despite the magnitude and intensity of this disaster, the *Titanic* story is undeniably alluring. In fact, the *Titanic Historical Society* was originally called "Titanic Enthusiasts of America!" The name of the group was changed only after a *Titanic* survivor, Mrs. Irene Harris of New York City, remarked, "I mean really, who can be enthusiastic about a tragedy?" Strangely, though, we are.

   The Arts and Entertainment Channel, "A & E," on cable television began re-running its fabulous 1994 documentary on *Titanic*, and I was blown away by it. The documentary was narrated by David McCallum, best known for the "Man From U.N.C.L.E." television series, but it was a young McCallum who played *Titanic's* junior wireless officer Harold Bride in "A Night To Remember." His voice had grown rich with age and the narration of the A & E documentary is mesmerizing. Casting him as the narrator was a stroke of genius on someone's part. The documentary features commentary by Walter Lord and other leading *Titanic* historians and authors, and also combines recreations of survivor testimony with modern day interviews with the few remaining *Titanic* survivors, those who were children at the time. It made me crazy to know what Pat O'Keefe's experience was.

Since I was a boy growing up in the 1960's I had heard my father speak of his uncle, but I have a suspicious nature and I never fully believed the story about Pat O'Keefe being aboard the great lost ship. Anytime the subject of *Titanic* came up, my father would remind my siblings and I that he had an "Uncle Paddy" who was on the ship and survived. Having the normal curiosity of children, we would ask, "So, what happened?", but my father would have to stop right there because he didn't know any details. In fact, no one in the family could explain how he survived, and because of that my wife Mary thought it unwise for me to tell people that I had a male relative who survived the sinking when so many women and children perished. I certainly didn't want to believe that he got into a lifeboat at the expense of a woman or child. I later learned that many of the men who survived the sinking were regarded with suspicion for the rest of their lives, and some never spoke of *Titanic* for that reason. For those who did nothing wrong, life was cruel to them not once, but twice. My father had a vague recollection that his uncle may have helped someone else survive...a businessman who promised Pat a job for life on Wall Street. My Uncle Tommy Nolan, the oldest of Jack's children, said he had heard something about his uncle saving someone and added that his Uncle Pat offered to get him a job on Wall Street as a runner or messenger boy, but he declined. "That's all I remember," said Uncle Tommy who added that he later regretted not taking the job. It was all very fuzzy, so the first thing I did was visit the public library in Cornwall-On-Hudson, New York, where I have lived since 1995. I found the passenger list for *Titanic* in the back of Walter Lord's <u>A Night To Remember</u>. The names of those who were saved are printed in italics. As my thumb reached the next-to-last page of the list, I was deciding that the story about my great uncle was nothing more than a bit of blarney. I then received a jolt when I found that Pat O'Keefe's name, in italics, appears on the very last page of the list! That's because those who embarked at Queenstown, Ireland were the last to board the doomed liner. I was flipping through the pages so fast I didn't realize the list was separated into sections based on points of departure: Southampton, England, Cherbourg, France, and Queenstown, Ireland.

  I went back to my father, Bill Nolan, and started pumping him for information about Pat O'Keefe. I had so many questions. When was he born? When and how did he die? Where is he buried? What did he do for a living? And what became of his wife, the former Anna Nolan, my great aunt? My dad, 69 at the time of this writing, was only a little boy when Pat was still around. He could still picture "Uncle Paddy" in his mind, but knew few details of the man's life. He does remember that Pat always wore a black hat, and that he once offered my father a pony. My family lived in the crowded tenements of New York City's "Hell's Kitchen" neighborhood, where there was little room for people, much less barnyard animals! My father went running home to ask his mother and father if it would be alright if Uncle Paddy got him a pony. I can just imagine their reaction, and I have always suspected (being suspicious as I am) that Great Uncle Pat was just teasing my father. My dad insists, however, that the offer was genuine, and that Pat O'Keefe was the kind of a guy who would somehow know where you could get a free pony! My father settled for a fat rabbit, which he kept on the fire escape, a poor man's balcony in those days.

  I decided to stop doubting my father at this point and asked him to call his other brother, my Uncle Eddie, who, like Tommy, lives on Long Island, to see what he knew of Pat O'Keefe. Uncle Eddie recalls that when Pat O'Keefe smiled or laughed, his small eyes closed. It's a wonder he could ever smile again after that horrible night in 1912. Uncle Ed and my father remembered a pair of boxing gloves they had in the apartment when they were kids. When their Uncle Pat would come to visit my grandfather, they say Pat would sometimes give them some loose change and ask them to put on a boxing show! There was no harm done...just little boys swatting at each other with oversized padded gloves, but my father says with a laugh, "I went for the knockout!" My father also has a sister, my Aunt Anna, who was named after the Anna Nolan who married Pat O'Keefe, but she is the youngest and I was told she wouldn't remember much. Sadly, our group of Nolan's lost contact with the O'Keefe's long ago, and many of the family members who would know anything have died. I don't recall ever meeting any of the O'Keefe's during my childhood. Well, then, I thought, what about family photos? Any pictures of Pat O'Keefe? Nope! Not a one!

   Since I wasn't having much luck with the family, I hit the bookstores and the library and looked through every *Titanic* book I could find, but none contained stories or pictures of Great Uncle Pat. I then turned to the internet. I went online and looked through the various *Titanic* websites, but found no information on Pat

O'Keefe other than the passenger list, which I had already obtained from the old-fashioned source of the library. I wrote a letter to the *Titanic Historical Society* in Massachusetts, but received no reply.

One of the last photographs ever taken of *Titanic*. Patrick O'Keefe is now on board as *Titanic* sails away from Queenstown, Ireland.

Chapter Two: Wireless Messages

One night while online I received e-mail from a pen pal in Nova Scotia. Her name is Johanne Tournier, an attorney who operates "The WebWorld of Bela Lugosi," a website devoted to actor Bela Lugosi, one of my favorites. She had neglected to respond to an inquiry I made about Lugosi, and when she realized she had forgotten about it, she apologized and explained that she was all wrapped up in a *Titanic* chat group. I should have known she would be interested in *Titanic*, since there is a *Titanic* cemetery in Halifax, where the bodies of unclaimed victims were buried. Many could not afford the trip to Nova Scotia to claim their dead. Since Johanne was obviously interested in *Titanic*, I immediately e-mailed back and informed her that I was related to a *Titanic* survivor. Her reaction was "Wow!" and she began asking all sorts of questions I couldn't answer. She is a sharp lady, and her curiosity and enthusiasm rubbed off on me. I suddenly realized that it was up to me to find the answers. I even began to berate myself. "What's wrong with you, John? Pat O'Keefe was your great uncle and you don't know anything about him? Why don't you try to find out about him yourself, instead of expecting someone else to do it for you?" And so I told Johanne I would find out more about Pat O'Keefe. She referred me to Philip Hind's *Titanic* website, "Encyclopedia Titanica," where we both posted messages. It is a huge website, located at http://www.encyclopedia-titanica.org and is enough to satisfy anyone interested in *Titanic*, but, alas, at that time it contained no information on Pat O'Keefe. It is a heavily visited site, however, and a short time later, Johanne received a reply from George Behe, Titanic historian, author and former vice-president of the Titanic Historical Society. Mr. Behe quoted from his first book, Titanic: Psychic Forewarnings of a Tragedy:

"Patrick O'Keefe was a young Irish immigrant who planned to seek his fortune in America. He left his home in Waterford and headed for Queenstown, where he was to board *Titanic* when she touched there. He arrived on April 10, intending to spend the night in a hotel and then board *Titanic* the next day. That night, however, Patrick O'Keefe had an unsettling dream in which he saw *Titanic* going down in mid-ocean. It's not known how this dream affected O'Keefe's peace of mind or whether he took it as a serious portent of approaching danger. In any case, the young man decided to follow through with his plans to sail the next day, and he went on board *Titanic* on April 11. After *Titanic* struck the iceberg, Patrick O'Keefe stayed on board until the sea rolled over the forward end of the boat deck. He jumped overboard and managed to swim through the freezing water to an overturned lifeboat. He and a group of other swimmers spent the night balanced on top of this slowly-sinking refuge from death. O'Keefe was taken aboard another lifeboat in the morning and survived the disaster. After reaching New York, Patrick O'Keefe wrote a letter to his father in Ireland in which he mentioned his dream that *Titanic* would sink."

After the sinking of the *Titanic*, many people would claim they had a premonition of the disaster, so I was skeptical of Pat O'Keefe's dream. (I'm a terrible cynic!) I was, however, greatly impressed and relieved to learn how Pat O'Keefe had managed to survive. I had heard the stories of how at least one male passenger dressed as a woman in order to secure a place in a lifeboat. There were other stories of panic and cowardice. The order was women and children first, and there were enough lifeboats for only about half the passengers. I had always wondered how a male steerage passenger such as

Pat O'Keefe could have survived. The odds were very much against him. The overturned lifeboat that he managed to swim to in 28 degree water was *Collapsible B*, the lifeboat that was washed overboard before it could be properly launched. It was the boat that carried Second Officer Charles Lightoller, wireless operator Harold Bride, American Army Colonel Archibald Gracie, and first class passenger Jack Thayer, all very famous survivors who would testify at the hearings and write about their experience. They were later joined by Titanic's chief baker Charles Joughin, one of the last people to leave the ship, as he rode the stern down into the sea. In James Cameron's "Titanic," an actor playing the baker is seen holding on to the stern railing along with Leo DiCaprio and Kate Winslet as the ship goes down.

   A few days after receiving this news of Great Uncle Pat's survival, I received e-mail from Brian R. Meister, a Titanic Researcher and Genealogist from Columbia, South Carolina. I suddenly felt like a wireless operator receiving urgent messages! Mr. Meister informed me that Pat O'Keefe's *Titanic* ticket number was 368402, and that he was with two young Englishmen, Victor Sunderland and Edward Dorking, when the *Titanic* went down. Mr. Meister wrote that all three men told the same, identical story of leaping together from the stern, and swimming to the overturned boat. All three survived. It's not certain, but they may have been roommates. According to an interview Sunderland gave to the *Cleveland Plain Dealer* in Ohio (where he settled), he was bunked in Section G, three decks below the main deck and close to the bow, where the ship struck the iceberg. Sunderland and his roommates were awake at the time, which was shortly before midnight. They were talking and smoking. Because of where they were situated, they had an early idea of the seriousness of the collision, but after going up on deck to investigate, they were sent back to their cabin by a steward who told them it was nothing serious. Fortunately, they stayed awake long enough to see the water coming in under their door and they left the cabin again. Dorking, who traveled to Illinois after the disaster, told the *Bureau County Republican* of Princeton that he was in the music room playing cards at the time of the accident, and was thrown from the bench he was sitting on when *Titanic* hit the iceberg. Both Sunderland and Dorking reported seeing chunks of ice on the forward deck, and both told the same story of trying to go back to their cabin again to get their life belts. They were unable to do so because their cabin was filling up with water. This leads me to believe that Pat O'Keefe did not have a life belt when he made the jump, but he was probably able to swim faster without one.

I tried to imagine what it was like. I've been on small boats many times, but I've only been on one steamship voyage: my honeymoon cruise to Bermuda in 1981 aboard the *S.S. Volendam*. I remember the lifeboat drill, and two minor incidents. We encountered a storm at sea and I couldn't believe that a large cruise ship could be tossed about so! There was so much seasickness that the ship ran out of dramamine, and the crew offered passengers golden delicious apples as a substitute! When we arrived at Bermuda, the ship ran aground. There were no injuries, but the Captain was fined.

Mr. Meister later sent me a transcript of Pat's letter to his father, which was published in a Waterford newspaper in 1912:

"April 23, 1912

Dear Father:

I write to you these few lines to let you know that I am safe and feeling fine. Don't worry for me, for I am going to start work in the morning for $12 a week. (Not bad for a shipwrecked man). Dear father, I am sure you felt downhearted when you heard the *Titanic* was lost. I dreamt myself she was going down before I left Queenstown, and I thought to sell my passage note for 7 pounds, but then I thought if I went back to Waterford again, the boys would be laughing at me. I lost everything I had on the *Titanic*, but thank God that my life is spared.

Hoping yourself and all the children are well as I myself am at present.

Your loving son,

Patrick"

A letter Pat O'Keefe wrote to an unidentified friend was also published:

"Dear Chum,

I write you a few lines to let you know I am all right after a rough trip. You might say I was a lucky one to get away that night. I will remember Sunday, April 14th at 12 o'clock midnight for a long time, but everything is now all right. Thank God, and I am starting to work in the morning. When I get home, I will never travel again. That night frightened me. I felt fine as silk and a cool head saved me for I and two London fellows got away on a raft and were picked up by the *Carpathia*. I was the only man from Waterford on her, and I am glad of that, too. I lost everything I had in her but my life. I have that yet. Excuse me for not writing longer as I am writing a number of letters to send across the pond.

Your old chum,

Pat Keefe"

   I was touched by the letters, and could relate to Pat losing all of his worldly possessions. In February, 1979, after only a few months in my first job as a radio announcer at a small station in Amsterdam, New York, my apartment burned to the ground and I lost everything. The early morning fire started in an adjoining apartment and spread to mine while I slept. If the landlord had not pounded on my door to awaken me, I would likely have died of smoke inhalation. My mother and father came to visit me after the fire, and my mother cried when she saw the ruins of where I had lived.

The overturned lifeboat on which Pat O'Keefe and 27 other survivors spent the night. Crewmen from the *Mackay-Bennett* are seen trying to salvage it. The *Mackay-Bennett* was sent to retrieve bodies.

Chapter Three: Face to Face with Pat O'Keefe

After learning of Pat O'Keefe's experience on *Titanic*, I found out that a photo of him did exist! Uncle Eddie remembered that his daughter, my cousin Patricia, (We always called her "Patty Girl.") had a book with a photo of Pat O'Keefe in it, but that the photo was not very clear. The blurry photo appears in Titanic: Triumph and Tragedy, by John Eaton and Charles Haas. I headed off to Barnes & Noble, found the book, and finally came face-to-face with Patrick O'Keefe. I called my cousin and asked how she found out there was a published photo of him. She told me her husband, Don McMahon, knew of her relation to Pat O'Keefe and her great interest in *Titanic*, so he routinely bought various books on the subject as gifts for her. Patty Girl told me that she too was frustrated by the lack of information about Pat O'Keefe and she recalled that one relative even told her that Pat was on the *Lusitania*! Neither she nor her husband knew that the Eaton and Haas book contained the photo, and Patty was stunned to find it when she read the book. His photo appears alongside those of three other third class passengers. The caption reads: "Among those enjoying *Titanic's* superior third class accommodation are Eileen and Neal McNamee, Patrick O'Keefe and August

Wennerstrom..." The photo credit reads: "Authors' Collection." I wondered how Eaton and Haas had come into possession of the photo of Pat, and I wrote a letter to them in care of their publisher. In the back of the book there is another version of the passenger list. It confirms that Pat O'Keefe was on *Collapsible B* and gives his age at the time of the disaster as 22. Since the tragedy occurred in 1912, it was safe to assume Pat O'Keefe was born in 1890. Okay, now we're getting somewhere!

   Pat lived on *Titanic* for four days, and as the saying goes, "It was great while it lasted!" Third class accommodations were indeed superior. Although *Titanic* was built with first class luxury in mind, third class passengers were well taken care of, since the booming steerage trade was the bread and butter of the steamship companies. A flood of immigration preceded the Great War, and there was still competition for passengers, despite J.P. Morgan's attempts to corner the market. Third class passengers were treated to dinner selections such as roast pork, beefsteak and kidney pie, fricassee rabbit with bacon, corned beef and cabbage, boiled mutton, ling fish (a popular food fish from the waters of northern Europe), and, of course, roast beef. Dinner came with vegetables, breads, fruits, coffee and tea. Many third class travelers probably never ate so well!

After finally catching a glimpse of Pat O'Keefe, I received an interesting e-mail message from Sinead Williams from Melbourne, Australia. "I'm becoming quite the man of the world," I thought to myself! Sinead had seen my posting on the internet and introduced herself as the great-niece of John Collins, an assistant cook in the first class galley on *Titanic*. Collins, from Belfast, Ireland, was only 17 at the time of the disaster and was on a ship for the first time in his life. He testified at the disaster hearings and told the heartbreaking story of how a child he was carrying was washed out of his arms and lost when a wave knocked him from the ship in *Titanic's* final hour. Collins survived by swimming to the very same overturned collapsible as Pat O'Keefe. When I told Sinead that I finally found a photo of Pat O'Keefe, she asked if I had seen any photos of John Collins. Her grandmother, Kathleen Collins, passed away in 1993 and her house was destroyed by fire. All of the family photos were lost in the blaze, and Sinead does not have a single picture of her great uncle. I looked through the Eaton and Haas book, and every other *Titanic* book I could find, but saw no photos of John Collins. Sinead put me in touch with Harry Holstine of Sacramento, California, who knew some O'Keefe's in

Waterford, Ireland. After checking with Harry, I learned that the O'Keefe's he knew were not related to my Pat O'Keefe. O'Keefe, of course, is a common name in Ireland. Harry was still interested in the Pat O'Keefe story though, and commented that it was a pity that Pat never got the kind of attention that people like Colonel Gracie and Second Officer Lightoller received. The attention they received was not undeserved, as both men worked very hard that awful night and their survival was nothing short of miraculous, but it is not surprising that a lowly steerage passenger would escape attention. I later put Sinead in touch with another *Titanic* researcher, Senan Molony of Dublin, Ireland, who told her of a book containing a photo of John Collins.

    I went back online to see if there was anything new at "Encyclopedia Titanica." There was. The site added a list of all the *Titanic* Societies, including the *Irish Titanic Historical Society*, which I had not seen before. It is based in Cork City, in the south of Ireland. Since Pat O'Keefe was from Waterford in the south, I thought this would be a good source to contact. I visited their website and e-mailed their contact person, Noel Ray, and inquired about Pat O'Keefe. Noel referred me to Dr. Andy Bielenberg, who, in turn, referred me to an Irish newspaper, *The*

Munster Express, which ran an article about Pat O'Keefe in February, 1998. Using my on-line service provider's search engine, I found the paper and the article! The report by Paul Collins is titled "Spring Garden Alley Man Was *Titanic* Hero." Wow! Not only was Pat O'Keefe <u>not</u> a cowardly female impersonator, he was a hero! The title of the article refers to an address in Ireland, No. 2 Spring Garden Alley, Waterford City, where the O'Keefe family lived in 1912. The paper quotes Father Michael Kenny, a priest who visited *Titanic* survivors at St. Vincent's Hospital in New York after they were brought there from the rescue ship *Carpathia*. Father Kenny was the Associate Editor of a New York Catholic weekly newspaper and wrote an article on the *Titanic* disaster. His article states:

"An act of heroism was performed by Patrick O'Keefe, a Waterford boy, who, plunging into the sea from the steerage deck, managed to capture a collapsible raft, on which he pulled, first, an Englishman from Southampton, then a Guernsey Islander, and after that, with the assistance of those he had already rescued, some twenty other men and women, who were finally landed safely on board the *Carpathia*. O'Keefe's success in rescuing lives after he assumed absolute command of the raft was one of the many providential avenues of escape provided for the steerage passengers of which I heard many recitals during my visit to St. Vincent's Hospital."

Although it is believed Pat jumped from the ship with fellow steerage passengers Dorking and Sunderland, they apparently did not arrive at the upturned lifeboat at the same time. The "Englishman from Southampton" was undoubtedly a crew member, since most of the survivors on Collapsible B were English crew members and most listed their address as Southampton, which served as the base for these seagoing men. A "Guernsey Islander" is someone from the isle of Guernsey, one of the Channel Islands in the English Channel. Although I was unable to find any record of a Collapsible B survivor from Guernsey, he too was likely a member of the crew, since some of the Southampton boys were not originally from that sailor town. In my check of survivor listings, I found only one male Guernsey islander who survived the sinking. He was Joseph Duquemin, a third class passenger who jumped from the ship and swam to Collapsible D, the last boat to be properly launched from *Titanic*. Since Pat O'Keefe told his father he got away on "a raft," it doesn't sound like he was on *Collapsible D* with Duquemin.

Duquemin's claim of being in the water was regarded with suspicion, but his legs were so badly frostbitten they had to be amputated. I guess that wasn't enough proof that he was in the frigid waters of the North Atlantic. The stories told by male passengers, from J. Bruce Ismay on down to the steerage men, were not always well received. While crew members could always say they were ordered to man a lifeboat by an officer, male passengers were suspected of rushing the boats, using their superior size and strength to push their way ahead of the women and children. Lifeboat commanders testified at the disaster hearings that this was not the case, but doubt and mistrust lingered.

My excitement about Pat's heroism was tempered by Father Kenny's mention of women. I knew from my research that no women were rescued from *Collapsible B* when morning came. In fact, only one woman was known to go down with *Titanic* and survive. Mrs. Rosa Abbott of East Providence, Rhode Island, a third class passenger who boarded *Titanic* at Southampton, swam to *Collapsible A* as it floated off the sinking *Titanic*. *Collapsible A* nearly sank as well, since the boat's collapsible canvas sides were not raised. Mrs. Abbott was transferred to *Collapsible D* during the night by Fifth Officer

Harold Lowe, the only lifeboat commander to go back for survivors. Mrs. Abbott could take no joy in her rescue, as she lost two teenage sons who jumped with her as *Titanic* went down. I have two sons of similar age, and I can picture the Abbotts trying to survive together as a family. It is horrible to think of how she must have felt when she found herself in a lifeboat without her boys.

   I decided to put aside the discrepancy about women being rescued, and simply enjoy the report of Great Uncle Pat's heroism. After all, discrepancies between survivor accounts were nothing new in the *Titanic* disaster. Some said they believed *Titanic* broke in two, while others said it went down intact. The debate was not settled until 1985 when Dr. Robert Ballard found the two pieces of *Titanic*. There have been many wild stories about *Titanic* through the years, including various sightings of Captain Smith during and after the sinking, much like the Elvis sightings following the death of the King of Rock 'n Roll. I later learned that Pat's companion Edward Dorking said he saw a woman on the overturned lifeboat while he was still struggling in the water. Not everyone who made it to the boat lasted the night.

   I was happy to find that the *Munster Express* article also named Pat O'Keefe's surviving Irish relatives. The paper interviewed Mrs. Lily Roche of Waterford, a niece of Pat O'Keefe. A grand-nephew, Noel Butler, also lives in Waterford, and told the paper that Pat O'Keefe was related to the O'Keefe, Roche, Butler and Hodgers families.

The *Munster Express* also mentioned Pat's premonition of the shipwreck, which I now believe. This incredible journey to the past has taught me to believe. I was reminded of my own trip to Ireland in 1996 with my wife Mary and three children, Jonathan, Kaitlin and Daniel, and Mary's parents, Maurice and Bridget McKenna, both born and raised in the north of Ireland. I do not like to fly, and in the days before the trip I thought about what it would be like to be in a plane that is going down. We boarded an Aer Lingus flight at Kennedy Airport on July 17, 1996. Our plane was late taking off, but everything seemed to go smoothly. We didn't learn until the next day that half an hour after we took off from JFK, TWA Flight 800 exploded behind us, killing all on board.

This photo of Pat appeared in the *Cork Examiner* in 1912, and was used many years later in the book, Titanic: Triumph and Tragedy.

Chapter Four: Back to Ireland!

In his reply to me, Dr. Bielenberg suggested I try to contact Lily Roche and he also referred me to Mary Broderick, a *Titanic* researcher specializing in the Queenstown passenger list. Since Dr. Bielenberg provided Mary's address in Cobh, as Queenstown is now known, I wrote to her first. She very kindly responded with a hand-written letter, but I learned nothing new, except for the fact that a *Titanic* monument was to be unveiled in Cobh on July 7, 1998.

Although the *Munster Express* did not provide a complete address for Mrs. Roche, I decided to take a chance and write her a letter as well. Along with my "snail mail" address, I provided my e-mail address, in the hope of getting a quicker response. Much to my surprise and delight, I got a reply. Bravo Irish Postal Service! Once again the internet also played a part, as Lily's son Sean had internet access and sent me an e-mail message.

Lily was as excited as I was, and sent me a color copy of a beautiful portrait of Pat O'Keefe's entire family. The portrait shows Pat, his parents John and Catherine, and seven siblings: Johnny, Jimmy, Lily's mom Ellen, Susan, Mollie, Eddie and Arthur. It was taken around 1909, (Of course, the color was painted on since there was no color film back then.) and although the picture had a few cracks from age, I now had a good look at Pat O'Keefe's face.

   Lily said she hoped to have the painting restored someday, but she was told it would cost at least fifty pounds, and she is a widow living on a fixed income. I was a little short of funds myself at the time, having lost my job at a radio station after fifteen years of service. The station was sold and the new owner made budget cuts. Well, that's show business! (I have since been re-hired.) I still felt a little guilty about Lily spending money to have the painting copied and mailed overseas to me, so I dug up twenty-five pounds left over from my trip to Ireland and sent it to her. I had tried to exchange the money when I got back to the states, but the rate was poor and the banks also charged fees for changing the money, so I just held on to it. Lily put the meager sum to great use! She paid for several record searches that gave us important dates in the life of Pat O'Keefe. Pat's parents, John O'Keefe and Catherine Fitzgerald were married October 26th, 1887 by Father Thomas Dowley in St. Patrick's Parish. Patrick was born July 11, 1890 and was baptised two days later on July 13th by Father Patrick Sheehan at Cathedral Church. The birth registry listed the O'Keefe's address at the time as Little Michael Street,

Waterford, and John O'Keefe's profession was listed as "labourer." I learned that John O'Keefe later became a newspaper office manager whose trucks delivered most of the newspapers in the south of Ireland. Lily told me Pat worked with his father for a while in the newspaper business.

   My son Daniel was born on July 12th, so he shares an astrological sign with Pat O'Keefe: Cancer, the sign of the crab. Since *Titanic* sank in April of 1912, I realized that Pat was 21 at the time of the disaster, not 22 as listed in the Eaton and Haas book, but I'm sure they simply rounded off his age. Speaking of the Eaton and Haas book, I received another package from Lily that contained a large photo of Pat in a full standing pose that looked strangely familiar. After closely examining Pat's face in the photo, I realized that it was a clear copy of the photo from the book, although the fuzzy picture in the book was cropped to look like a head-shot. The mystery was not solved until months later when I finally received a reply to my letter from Jack Eaton himself. Mr. Eaton explained that the photo was published many years ago in an Irish newspaper, the *Cork Examiner*, and since the copyright had expired, he and his partner Charles Haas listed such items as being from "Authors' Collection." Mr. Eaton sent me a copy of the photo as it appeared in the newspaper, but he didn't know that I already had a much better copy thanks to Lily. The portrait of Pat was taken at the Poole Photographic Studio in Waterford in 1912, the year of the disaster. When the studio went out of business in 1954, the family of A.H. Poole sold its collection of 65,000 original glass negatives to the National Library of Ireland. The portrait of Pat is included in that collection, and so my great uncle has a place in the National Library of Ireland! Mr. Eaton also sent me a brief summary of what was known about Pat at the time of the *Titanic* sinking. Most of it I had already seen by this time, but the new piece of information was Pat's first American address: 460 West 38th Street in New York, an apartment he shared with his cousin John Phelan. This was significant to me because it explained how Pat got to know my grandfather, who lived at 514 West 44th Street at the time. I knew that Pat must have lived in the same "Hell's Kitchen" neighborhood at one time, and this was now confirmed.

   By the way, Mr. Eaton would have responded much sooner, but his publisher was late in forwarding mail from readers.

   According to Lily Roche, Pat O'Keefe was indeed a very powerful swimmer, and often went for a Christmas Day swim in the River Suir in Waterford with his little brother, Arthur, when they were young. This would explain Pat's ability to survive the frigid waters of the North Atlantic. Lily's mother Ellen told her that Pat's father would scold him for taking his little brother in the river because of the strong current. I remembered the strong current in the Hudson River when I swam from a dock at 40th street in New York City when I was a boy. It was no longer in use and unguarded, so my brother Billy and I swam there with our friends. The old dock was just south of Pier 83, home of the Circle Line Sightseeing Cruiser. My parents would have been horrified if they had known. Not only was the current strong, the water was very dirty. It was salty, though, as it contained water from the Atlantic Ocean. One day we took a walk to the dock and saw police cars and other emergency vehicles. Another boy disappeared there, and was presumed drowned.

   Much to the regret of his family, Pat O'Keefe refused to cross the ocean again after the *Titanic* disaster, and never returned to his native Ireland. Brothers Arthur and Eddie would later join Pat in America, and sister Mollie may have come as well, but Lily's mom Ellen never got to see her brother again. Lily told me that Pat passed away in the late 1930's, at the age of 47. My father was born in 1930, and if Pat died around 1937, that means my Dad was only 7 years old when his uncle died. That would explain why he remembers little! I asked him if he had any idea why Pat died so young. He didn't know, but later, after some phone calls, we learned that my father's sister Anna did remember something of Pat O'Keefe. She was told years later that Pat died as a result of some kind of mishap, and was dead on arrival at the hospital. I wrote to Lily again and asked if she knew how Pat died. While she did not know the exact cause of death, she said that he did indeed die unexpectedly while on a shopping trip at Christmas time in the 1930's. I was saddened to learn that Pat O'Keefe had a tragic, untimely death after all. An untimely death in the family was nothing new to the O'Keefe's. Lily explained that Pat's mother died shortly after the family portrait was taken in 1909. She was only 37! I was reminded of Pat's letter to his father in 1912. He signed off with "Hoping yourself and all the children are well as I myself am at present." I had wondered why Pat didn't mention his mother. She was already gone. I would later learn of other premature deaths in the O'Keefe family.

   It was heartwarming, though, to learn that Pat's daughter Margaret made the voyage to Ireland in 1982 and visited Lily Roche. A family reunion did occur, and part of Pat O'Keefe finally made it back to Ireland! I wondered what it would be like to get Pat O'Keefe's surviving relatives in Ireland together today with those in America, including my dad, his brothers Tommy and Eddie, their sister, now Anna Morgan, and, of course, Ed O'Keefe and his family. After Margaret's death in 1988, Lily lost Ed O'Keefe's address and, like the Nolan's many years earlier, she too lost contact with the O'Keefe's in America. I decided to make the extra effort and try to find Ed O'Keefe myself! At the very least, I hoped to repay Lily Roche for her help by finding Ed for her. I also wanted to see my father and his siblings together again with their cousin Ed before it is too late.

The O'Keefe Family (circa 1909) Top: Ellen; next row, left to right: John, James, Patrick; middle: parents John and Catherine; bottom: Susan, Mollie, Edward (in Catherine's lap) and Arthur (in sailor suit).

A close-up of Pat from the original negative of the family portrait. Without the painted-on colors, Pat's face is more clearly seen.

Lily Roche, daughter of Pat's sister, Ellen.

Chapter Five: Detective Work

No one in my family had any idea where Ed lived, so I had to play detective. I went online again and checked AOL's "White Pages" directory and found phone numbers for twenty-seven Edward O'Keefe's in New York State. "Well, that's not too bad," I thought. So, if I have to make twenty-seven phone calls, it's a small price to pay if I find Ed. I was a little nervous about calling strangers and explaining that I'm looking for a lost relative. I get so annoyed by telemarketers calling me all the time with various offers, so I was sure people would think I was some kind of scam artist. I procrastinated a bit, and while I put things off I received another letter from Lily. She sent me copies of some snapshots Margaret had sent her of Ed, Margaret and some of Ed's children and grandchildren. "At least now I know what Ed looks like," I told myself as I looked at a snapshot. When I turned the photo over, I saw Lily's note: "His wife's name is Patricia." It was then I got the idea to check the "White Pages" for Patricia O'Keefe's and match them up with those Ed O'Keefe's with the same phone number. To my surprise and relief, I narrowed the search down to two! There were two Edward P. O'Keefe's with a Patricia O'Keefe at the same address and phone number.

On a Sunday afternoon in July when I was home alone I decided to make the calls. I thought about what I was going to say, took a deep breath and dialed the first number. I got an answering machine and left a lame message. I tried the other number and a gentleman answered.

"Edward O'Keefe?" I asked.

"Yes." he answered.

"My name is John Nolan and I'm looking for an Edward O'Keefe that I'm related to, but I've never met him. Was your father's name Patrick?"

"Yes."

"Was your mother's name Anna?"

"Yes."

At this point I felt I had to put this Mr. O'Keefe to some kind of test. I had to be sure!

"Was your father famous for something?"

"Well, I don't know if you can call it famous, but my father was on the *Titanic*."

I couldn't believe it! Two phone calls and I found him! The first thing I learned from Ed O'Keefe was that his father never told him of his experience on *Titanic*!   Ed said he was very close to his father, who took him everywhere, including "every fish and chip joint in Manhattan," but Pat never told his son about the historic disaster. Perhaps he intended to talk about it when Ed was older. I still felt a bit awkward, but Ed put me right at ease. He told me he remembered my father "Billy" very well, and that my grandfather "Jack" was a favorite of Pat O'Keefe's. This made me feel good, but I also wished that I had gotten to know my grandfather a little better. I was only 12 when he died, and he suffered terribly from emphysema and asthma in the latter part of his life and understandably was not very playful. On the other hand, I was shy and quiet as a child and did not reach out. My maternal grandfather, James "Papa" McTiernan would literally "reach out." He used to grab us grandkids and rub his stubble against our cheeks to tickle us.

  We were told Grandpa Nolan fought in World War One and endured enemy gas attacks that caused breathing problems that got worse over the years. That turned out to be another family story that wasn't quite true. My Uncle Tommy told me that Jack did serve in the Army during the first World War, but he worked on an ammunition train. My grandfather delivered the bullets! Uncle Tommy said his father's breathing problems were the result of working in a chemical plant back when there was little or no worker protection, and he was forced to breathe harmful fumes. The way I remember Grandpa Nolan, it was hard to imagine him as the cheery sort of fellow who used to pal around with Pat O'Keefe. My grandmother, Emma, though, had a great sense of humor and was always laughing. Ed O'Keefe said he remembered how cheerful she always was.

"So, I understand you have a couple of daughters," I said to Ed. "A couple?" he replied. "I have four lovely daughters!" "Wow! It really has been a long time!" I said. My father and his siblings have been out of touch with the O'Keefe's for so long that they missed two of Ed's daughters! The girls, in age order, are "Peachy" (Patricia, after mom), Colleen, Margie and Jackie.

I mentioned to Ed that Lily Roche had told me he and his wife, the former Patricia Huson, were due to celebrate their 50th wedding anniversary in August, and I congratulated him on his upcoming milestone. He thanked me and very graciously invited me to the family celebration that was planned for the occasion. I was anxious to meet him so I accepted. After chatting with him on the phone for a few minutes I got around to the unpleasant task of asking about his father's death. "Oh, no," he said. "It wasn't 1937. It was 1939. I remember distinctly because it was the year the World's Fair came to New York."

Ed told me his father suffered a fatal heart attack while waiting outside a meat market where wife Anna was doing some shopping. Anna could see a crowd gathering outside the store, and when she went out to investigate, she found her husband lying in the street. He was rushed to St. Luke's Hospital, where he was pronounced dead on arrival. It was mid-December of 1939, so Pat was 49 years old when he died. Ed was 14 at the time. My father was 9, not 7 as we thought, so his claim of remembering his uncle became more reasonable.

I told Ed that I had pictures of his dad from when he was a young man in Ireland and would bring him copies. I explained how I had found Lily Roche before finding him, and how excited she would be to learn that I had located him. On the subject of pictures, Ed told me had very little left of his father. When Pat O'Keefe died, his wife Anna was only 34 years old, fifteen years his junior. She later remarried, which is perfectly understandable, but Ed said the man she married, Andy Bartlett, was a very disagreeable fellow. It seems Anna was the only one who liked the man, and no one would visit when he was around. This continued throughout Anna's life, and when she died in 1968, no one went to Bartlett's home to retrieve Anna's personal things, including a steamer trunk that contained family photos and Pat O'Keefe's few worldly possessions. "What became of that steamer trunk?" I wondered.

I asked Ed if it would be alright with him if I visited his dad's grave. "Certainly," he replied and told me his father was buried at Gate of Heaven Cemetery in Hawthorne, New York. It is a Catholic cemetery owned by St. Patrick's Cathedral in New York City. After telling my father the good news that I had found his long lost cousin, we decided to first go and pay our respects to his late uncle. It was a hot and humid day when we traveled to Gate of Heaven. It was a bit of a hike to Pat's grave from the parking lot, so my father had to go slowly because of the heat. I went ahead to locate the grave. Pat is buried in section 48, plot 246, grave 10. We found it and discovered that his wife Anna and daughter Margaret are buried with him. There is no mention of *Titanic* on the gravestone. We took a few pictures, said our prayers and left for home to await our meeting with Ed.

My father was not comfortable about "crashing" Ed and Pat's anniversary party, so I wrote Ed a letter and told him we didn't wish to intrude or impose and would be willing to meet him another time in the near future. What Ed didn't know was that his daughters had planned a celebration that was on a larger scale than the quiet dinner he was expecting at a restaurant. I received a call from his daughter Margie and we spent a little time getting acquainted. She never met her grandfather Pat O'Keefe, of course, but she was very close to her grandmother, and still had Anna's copy of the Bible. Inside the Bible were funeral prayer cards for assorted Nolan's, but she never knew who the people were. Now she was talking to one of their descendants! Margie explained that she and her sisters had invited Ed's former co-workers to the anniversary party and planned other surprises, so we agreed that it would be better to meet the O'Keefe's in a more quiet setting. We set a date of Friday, August 28, 1998 to get together at Margie's house in Mahopac, New York.

Before the reunion I received an e-mail message from another O'Keefe on August 16th:

"Hi, Mr. Nolan,

You found us before we found you, but my name is Jackie O'Keefe, daughter of Edward P. O'Keefe. We celebrated my parents' 50th anniversary yesterday and it was just fantastic. I understand you will be getting together with them this month sometime. It's very nice to have found a long lost relative. Hey, take care. I got your name off the *Titanic* list encyclopedia. Jackie."

I immediately e-mailed Jackie and asked her to call me John. I then remembered to e-mail Lily's son Sean and tell him the good news that I had found Ed O'Keefe. Sean quickly replied, with Mom Lily sitting by his side at the computer, excitedly giving him messages for me. Lily later sent me more research. I had asked about Pat O'Keefe's education and Lily found that Pat started school at the Sisters of Charity School for Boys and Girls on Parnell Street in Waterford, and was later taught by the Christian Brothers at De-La-Salle School on Stephen's Street. It all sounded very familiar. I too received a Catholic education in the same way. Boys and girls are first taught by the nuns, from kindergarten through third grade, then, at fourth grade the boys and girls are separated, with the girls continuing with the Sisters, and the boys being taught by the Brothers. Not much changed in many, many years. Lily told me Pat left school at the age of 15 to go to work, which was common for Ireland of that time. I stayed in school but took a part time job at age 15 at a small Irish-owned grocery store across the street from my apartment building in New York, where I listened to tales of Ireland spun by the old Irish gentlemen who worked there. One of my co-workers, Pete Kelly, an amazing 70 year old man who worked harder than most of the teenagers I knew, told me then that he left home at 16 to go find work in Dublin. In Ireland of that time, you didn't start work at an early age just to earn spending money for yourself or to give Mom and Dad a few pounds to help out. You were quite often expected to be on your own by then.

Lily sent me a copy of Grandpa John O'Keefe's death certificate, which contained another surprise for me. Pat O'Keefe and his father died in the same year, 1939, both from heart problems! John died in June, 1939 at age 70, and son Pat followed in December at age 49.

While researching the O'Keefe's, I also got a chance to find out about the Nolan roots. I knew from my visit to Ireland in 1996 that the Nolan clan had its beginnings in County Carlow, but I didn't know exactly where my modern family came from. Don McMahon, my cousin's husband, did some research on the Nolan's and found that my Great Grandfather James Nolan was born in County Kilkenny, Ireland in 1854, the son of John Nolan (another one!) and the former Mary Tracy. James married Catherine

Collier (also spelled "Collyer") of Waterford. Kilkenny and Waterford are neighboring counties. Since I am only related to Pat O'Keefe of Waterford through marriage, I was happy to learn that I do have some Waterford blood in my veins! James Nolan came to America in 1888. That was before Ellis Island became the gateway to America, so Great-Grandpa Jimmy must have come through Castle Garden, the immigration station at the Battery in lower Manhattan. Great Grandma Catherine came over the following year. It was not unusual for immigrant men to come first, establish themselves in a trade, and then send for their families when they'd saved up enough money. James Nolan died of a cerebral hemorrhage at the age of 79 in 1933. At the time he was living in New York City with his daughter Anna and her husband...Patrick O'Keefe.

    Ed O'Keefe later told me the story of how Great-Grandpa Jimmy died. It's sad, but at the same time it is comical in the tradition of dark Irish humor. Jimmy's wife Catherine had already passed away and he moved in with the O'Keefe's, as did his son, Mickey, or "Uncle Mickey" to little Ed. It was the time of the Great Depression and many were left homeless. One day Grandpa Jimmy heard Uncle Mickey leaving the apartment. Still spry, he raced out to the hallway to catch Mickey as he headed down the stairs. "Mickey! Bring me back a beer!" he cried out as he reached the top of the stairs. Unfortunately, Grandpa couldn't stop and tumbled down the stairs and hit his head. He died later at the hospital. If not for the fall, he probably would have lived to be 100!

Pat O'Keefe's daughter Margaret.

Pat's son, Edward.

There is no mention of Titanic at Pat's grave.

Chapter Six: Family Reunion

The day finally came and I brought my father and then 15 year old son Jonathan along so that we would have three generations of Nolan's represented. I also brought a framed color copy of the O'Keefe family portrait sent to me by Lily Roche. When we arrived we were quite impressed with Margie's lovely home in the country. It was beautifully landscaped and included an in-ground swimming pool. We were met in the driveway by Ed's wife Pat, who told us that she and Ed had just arrived themselves. We went inside and at long last my father got to see the cousin he hadn't seen in nearly fifty years! After a round of handshakes and hugs with Ed and Pat, daughters Margie and "Peachy," Margie's husband Bill and Peachy's young son, another "Eddie," I showed off the color portrait of the O'Keefe clan from Ireland and identified those pictured. I also brought copies of several other photos of the O'Keefe's supplied by Lily. We then sat down and had lunch. Margie put out a great "spread" and it reminded my father of the times Uncle Pat came to visit. Dad said there was always lots of cold cuts and snacks, and a lot of smoking back then, and he and his brothers would snatch a few cigarettes and run off to have a smoke themselves!

During lunch I had to mention the story about the pony. Ed's eyebrows shot up! "My father was going to give YOU a pony?" he asked my father Bill. "He never offered ME a pony!" My father told him that he had to settle for the fat rabbit. "Now, wait a minute," said Ed as he remembered. "I had a rabbit! I always wondered what happened to it!" I'll bet Ed's mom Anna wanted to get rid of that rabbit, and asked hubby Pat to find someone to take it off their hands! My Dad asked Ed if he remembered the boxing gloves they used to play with. "Do I?" replied Ed. "You bet! Sister Margaret used to give me a shellacking with those gloves...until I got bigger!"

    I shared what I had learned of Pat O'Keefe's experience on *Titanic*, and Ed was glad to hear it because his father never told him anything about it. "My father was the original 'Quiet Man,'" quipped Ed, referring to the John Wayne movie. "He never said much about anything!" When I told Ed about his father's Christmas Day swims with brother Arthur, he remembered that his dad was indeed a strong swimmer. When Ed's family went to the shore, Pat would go off by himself and swim far from the beach, almost to the point where you could no longer see him from shore. While he never sailed the ocean again, Pat did not lose his love of the water and swimming. "But that was the only exercise he ever got," added Ed, who said his father's normal position was sitting back with his hands clasped behind his head and a cigarette dangling from his lips. He wouldn't even flick the cigarette ash until it had grown quite long, prompting son Ed to come running with an ashtray at times. Ed said his father worked all his life as an elevator "starter" at Number Two Rector Street, a large office building in lower Manhattan. My father, another elevator man, explained that an elevator starter is responsible for monitoring and directing elevator traffic flow, usually from a lighted console at a desk in the main lobby. While there is no doubt that the *Titanic* disaster took years off his life, Pat's desk job and everything else I learned about him made me think that his death at 49 was at least partly due to a sedentary lifestyle, fatty diet (Remember the meat market? I'll bet the fish and chips were greasy too!), smoking and, last but not least, keeping things bottled up inside.

   The O'Keefe's lived at 973 Columbus Avenue and later at 120 West 109th street in New York City, uptown from the Hell's Kitchen neighborhood of the Nolan's and a long way from Rector Street. Ed recalled that when his family was moving, brother-in-law and buddy Jack Nolan showed up with a horse and carriage to move their belongings! What a sight that must have been! It made me think of the lost steamer trunk. The little boy still inside of me fantasized about what treasures may have been inside. Perhaps the very clothes Pat wore when *Titanic* went down? Ed said he was sorry he didn't go back for the trunk when his mother passed away in 1968, and he's certain it was tossed out when Mr. Bartlett died some time later. I soon learned, however, that all was not lost!

First cousins Ed O'Keefe and Bill Nolan, reunited after nearly 50 years.

Chapter Seven: Cardboard Treasure Chest

Ed had brought with him a small cardboard box containing old photos and some of his father's personal papers. A short time earlier I showed Ed pictures of his father and grandfather he had never seen. I was then amazed when Ed showed me pictures of my great-grandfather James Nolan. I had never in my life seen what James Nolan looked like! I also got to see photos of my grandfather Jack and Pat's wife, my great aunt Anna Nolan. It was at that time that I learned that my great-grandfather lived with the O'Keefe's for many years, as did Anna's brother Mickey Nolan and various other family members from Anna's side. Although I know that back then times were very hard and many were without jobs and homes, a funny thought occurred to me. No wonder the O'Keefe's got away from the Nolan's! They were afraid we'd move in with them! We were the "poor relations!" Also in the box was a fragment of an old unidentified newspaper clipping about Pat O'Keefe that was published after his death. It contained the startling revelation that the *Titanic* voyage was not Pat's first trip to America, as I was led to believe. According to the article, Pat left for America three years before the *Titanic* disaster, and returned to Ireland in 1912 to spend a holiday with his father and siblings. His mother had passed away by this time. It seems Pat had planned to return to New York on the *Baltic*, but was persuaded by his brother James to transfer to the *Titanic* so that he could stay another week and spend Easter with the family in Ireland!

I later made a trip to the National Archives on Varick Street in Manhattan to try to find out just when Pat came to America. Census information and ships' passenger lists dating back many years are stored there and are available for public inspection. The staff was very helpful and after scanning a few reels of microfilm, I found the passenger list for the *S.S. Celtic*, which departed Queenstown, Ireland August 28, 1910 and arrived in New York on September 4th. Traveling third class were Pat O'Keefe, then age 20, and two uncles, Arthur and "Patsy" O'Keefe. Young Pat came over as a "non-immigrant alien" to work as a laborer. His first home in America was Uncle Arthur's apartment at 465 10th Avenue in Manhattan. My first home as a child was an apartment building a few blocks north, at 691 10th Avenue.

Since Pat had left Ireland before 1912, the family portrait taken around 1909 takes on added significance. Was it taken because Pat was about to leave for America, or because his mother was already dying? Or both?

Pat was only 19 when he first left home. Although I didn't go off to another country like Pat did, I too left home at 19 and got my first apartment in New York City, on the second floor of 503 West 47th Street, which turned out to be the last apartment lived in by Grandpa and Grandma Nolan before they moved to Brentwood on Long Island. It was just a weird coincidence to me back then, but now I wonder if author George Behe would find some psychic connections to the past.

Ed's box also contained a reprint of an article that appeared in the London *Daily Sketch* on May 7th, 1912, telling the story of Pat's dream about *Titanic* sinking. According to the article, when Pat's father, John O'Keefe, was first told the *Titanic* had gone down, he exclaimed: "Paddy is so lucky that if anyone is saved, he will be saved!"

As I sifted through the cardboard box like an archaeologist, I came across the funeral cards and death certificate for Pat O'Keefe. He died December 16, 1939 and the cause of death was listed as coronary thrombosis. Pat's death was so sudden and unexpected, there must have been a lot of confusion at the time, and the death certificate contains a few errors. Pat's age was given incorrectly twice, his date of birth was omitted, and the certificate stated that he was a

U.S. resident for 35 years, which must have been an estimate on Anna's part. Pat emigrated in 1910, so he was here in the U.S. for 29 years at the time he died. Noting the date, so close to December 25th, I said to Ed: "That must have been a terrible Christmas." "It was," he replied, looking down. Pat was a very organized fellow, and had purchased and wrapped the Christmas presents for his children weeks in advance. He had bought a football for Ed, who was 14 at the time. "Opening that package from my dad was the hardest thing I had ever done," Ed confessed.

Pat had also set aside money for the family to visit the 1939 World's Fair in New York. After a period of mourning, the fair was still open in 1940 so Anna decided to fulfill Pat's wishes and take the children to the fair, which featured such innovations as a thing called television! "Not only that," added Ed, "They had telephones with television monitors so you could see who you were talking to! They had us believing these things would be in every household in the very near future. That was 1940, and we still don't have them today!" (The webcam and things like Skype didn't come along until a few years later.)

Other interesting items Ed had found included his father's discharge papers from the Canadian Army! "I haven't a clue!" said Ed before I could even ask for an explanation. Patrick O'Keefe enlisted in the 110th regiment of the Canadian Expeditionary Force at Toronto, Ontario on July 3lst, 1917 and served in Canada until February 24, 1919 when his unit, the 5th battalion, was demobilized. He was a private. His discharge certificate describes him as 5' 6" in height, with dark complexion, hazel eyes and brown hair. Dark complexion? A Waterford man with a dark complexion? There must have been a lot of sunshine in Toronto.

  I found what I believed to be an explanation for Pat's Canadian military service in the form of his certificate for United States citizenship, which, by the way, lists his complexion as "fair." Pat O'Keefe did not become a U.S. citizen until July of 1939, the year he died! At the time he served in the Canadian military, during World War One, the Irish Republic had not yet been formed and so Pat's nationality was listed as "Great Britain." As a British subject, he would be expected to serve during a World War, but Pat would never cross the ocean again after *Titanic*, so he did his duty in Canada, a member of the British Commonwealth of Nations. My guess is that he took a train to Canada from New York. Another important consideration is the failed Easter Rebellion, an uprising of Irish nationalists in Dublin in 1916. The rebellion was put down in brutal fashion, and Britain executed 15 Irish nationalist leaders. It is very likely that this young Catholic man from Waterford would be opposed to serving with the English army a year later. A short time after I wrote this observation I received an e-mail message from Brian Cullen of Waterford, Ireland. Like me, Brian is related to the O'Keefe's through marriage. He contacted me on behalf of Mrs. Mary Collopy, a granddaughter of John O'Keefe, Pat's brother. Mary wanted to learn more about Pat O'Keefe and *Titanic*. Brian wrote, "My great aunt was Annie Carberry, who was married to John O'Keefe, who was Patrick's brother. They lived in Alexander Street in Waterford. John was killed in an ambush outside of Waterford in 1922 during the civil war in Ireland."

Pat's brother John was killed the same year as Irish Patriot Michael Collins, who was assassinated by members of the Sinn Fein party who were opposed to the peace treaty he negotiated with Great Britain. Although that treaty created the Irish Free State, it also divided Ireland and led to civil war. Only ten years after *Titanic*, the O'Keefe family was again caught in the middle of something both historic and tragic.

With the steamer trunk gone, I was sure there was nothing left from the time of *Titanic's* sinking in Ed O'Keefe's cardboard box of treasures. I was wrong!

This photo of Pat was taken for his U.S. citizenship papers in 1939. He died later that year.

Pat O'Keefe's wife, the former Anna Nolan.

Chapter Eight: The Settlement Offer

There in the box were two very old handwritten letters on the stationery of the Greeley Square Hotel Company on Madison Avenue in New York. The letters were discolored and very fragile. They were neither dated nor signed. One letter reads:

"Dear sir,

The attorneys for the steamship navigation company Ltd. think the company will give you transportation to Ireland, provided you will sign an agreement along the lines of the enclosed. In our opinion you should be willing to do this. If so, please sign and return it to us, and we will take the matter up further."

The second letter, the "agreement," reads as follows:

"Gentlemen,

In consideration of your supplying me with a third class (the word "ticket" crossed out) passage on one of your ships sailing within the next few weeks to Queenstown, I kindly agree not to institute suit against you in England on account of personal injuries or loss of baggage or otherwise by reason of the sinking of the *Titanic*. This letter is without prejudice to any rights under the claim heretofore filed by me in the proceedings for limitation of liability in this country or an independent suit in this country."

The handwriting is the same as the first letter. Now, I'm no handwriting expert and I've only seen Pat's signature, but the handwriting does look a little bit like Pat's. Why would his handwriting be on both letters? And why are the letters on hotel stationery and not White Star stationery or a law firm's stationery? My guess is that Pat transcribed the proposals to make himself a copy. I received another e-mail from Brian Cullen of Waterford that may have something to do with it:

"Hi, John. I have a small photocopy of an article taken from a newspaper which Mrs. Collopy (John O'Keefe's granddaughter) gave me. There is no date on the page but it looks like it is from a local newspaper. It reads as follows: 'Interesting item: The compiler of this column has in his possession an item which should be of interest to the curator of some museum, and he would be quite willing to donate it to anybody interested, like for instance, the local maritime museum. The item is a letter from some gentlemen (the name is undecipherable) who in the year 1912, was an executive of the White Star Line in New York, and the subject of the letter was a Waterford man, Patrick O'Keefe, son of the late John O'Keefe, Alexander Street (newspaper distributor), a survivor of the wreck of the *S.S. Titanic*, which sunk off the Grand Bank, Newfoundland, on April 18, 1912. Mr. O'Keefe sent the letter to his brother, the late Jimmy O'Keefe, Doyle Street, with the inscription written on the back, as follows: "Frame for safe keeping for some day it will be useful." '

So, perhaps Pat did transcribe the letters for his own records, and sent the originals to his brother Jimmy. I wish I knew who the columnist was who had the letter in his possession, and was willing to donate it. I would like to give it to Ed O'Keefe. Well, in any event, we can be certain that Pat O'Keefe did not accept the White Star offer. He never returned to Ireland.

Can it be that all they offered him was a return trip to Ireland?! A man loses all his worldly possessions, and very nearly his life as well, and they offer to send him back where he came from? It boggles the mind! These attorneys are only too happy to tell this young immigrant that this agreement will not affect his claims in America. What they probably didn't tell him was that under American law, the steamship company's liability was limited to the ship's salvage value plus monies paid by passengers and those sending cargo. Since only the lifeboats remained, the grand total came to about 97 thousand dollars. Legally, that amount was to be used to settle nearly 17 million dollars in claims! White Star attorneys were obviously more concerned with the company's liability in English courts, and offered free trips to convince survivors not to sue in England. It didn't matter to Pat O'Keefe, who found a job in New York and stayed for life, except for his stint in the Canadian military.

   I later learned that a record of Pat's claim against White Star still existed and was on file with all of the other claims at the National Archives on Varick Street in lower Manhattan. Author Jack Eaton put me in touch with Michael Findlay of the *Titanic International Society*, who in turn connected me with Robert Bracken of the Society. Mr. Bracken told me he had made copies of all the claims but he couldn't find Pat's, so I went to the Archives myself and got a copy. Pat was represented by the Wall Street firm of Harrington, Bigham and Englar. I had hoped to see an itemized list of the things

Pat lost on *Titanic*, but the claim only refers to lost "baggage and valuables" valued at 250 dollars. In addition to that amount, Pat asked for 10,000 dollars for his injuries from exposure and lost wages. Pat's legal claim is consistent with other accounts of what happened and states that "claimant was obliged to jump overboard to save his life. He was in the water a considerable period until rescued by one of the life-boats. During the time he was in the water and afterwards while in the life-boat, he suffered bitterly from the cold, and as a result of such exposure was made sick, sore, lame and disabled." The lawsuits dragged on until 1916 when a final settlement was signed, awarding a total of 663,000 dollars, a big improvement over the amount set by the "limitation of liability" law, but still much less than the total of claims. The settlement was to be divided among the claimants on a "pro rata" basis, or in proportion to the amount of each individual claim. Although I was certain that Pat received very little money, I still wanted to know just how much he got. I checked to see if the law firm that represented him was still around. After all, there are many very old law firms that are carried on from generation to generation. Sure enough, a search of the Yellow Pages revealed the firm is still in existence and still operating on Wall Street! The firm is now known as Bigham, Englar, Jones and Houston, and it has moved a short distance, from 64 Wall Street to 40 Wall Street. I gave them a call and was directed to Mr. Joseph Kilbourn, an attorney who has been with the firm some 50 years! Mr. Kilbourn was very familiar with *Titanic* and the firm's connection to the disaster, and he even wrote a paper on the subject and gave an address to the Bar Association on the matter. He gave me the sad news that the law firm's *Titanic* files were lost! According to Mr. Kilbourn, they were thrown away about 25 years earlier by someone at the firm who felt there was too much clutter! The firm had also done legal work on the *Lusitania* and *Andrea Doria* disasters, and those files were tossed away too! Mr. Kilbourn is still angry about it. It's hard to understand how documents of such great historical significance could be tossed out by some "neat freak" for the sake of tidying up and making some space! Mr. Kilbourn managed to hold on to a bound volume containing a summary of the 1916 settlement of the claims, but it does not provide an itemized accounting of who got what. There were 651 claimants splitting the 663 thousand dollars, for an average of slightly more than one thousand apiece. But the money wasn't split evenly, so a steerage passenger like Pat O'Keefe would be lucky to get a hundred bucks.

   Getting back to our visit with the O'Keefe's, the grownups chatted while my son Jonathan played Nintendo with Peachy's son, little Eddie, and then they went for a swim in Margie's pool. There was a bit of excitement when Margie's dogs joined the boys in the pool! After coffee and dessert, it was time to leave. Before heading out, we took a round of photos and exchanged addresses and phone numbers. There was one more surprise for us as we said our goodbyes. As my father was saying farewell to little Eddie, we were told that Peachy adopted the boy from Romania. My sister Joanne and her husband Bob McDermott also adopted a boy, Joshua, from Romania! And so we are connected in yet another way. I went home with a wealth of new information and began to write the Pat O'Keefe story.

   To get a feel for how the O'Keefe's lived, I traveled to New York City and visited Pat's old neighborhood in upper Manhattan. I was happy to find that both of his old apartment buildings were still standing and in pretty good shape! The O'Keefe's lived only a couple of blocks from Central Park, which must have been great for Ed and Margaret when they were kids. There is a subway station at 109th Street and Central Park West, which is undoubtedly where Pat O'Keefe caught the train to his job at Rector Street in lower Manhattan. St. Luke's Hospital is within walking distance, along with the beautiful Cathedral of St. John the Divine. What a great neighborhood Pat found for his family!

The following summer I visited Ed at his home in upstate New York. This time I brought my wife and all three children, along with my father again. My mother, Kathleen, couldn't make the trip because she was caring for my ailing older sister, also named Kathleen. Ed and his wife Pat have a beautiful lakefront home with a dock and a pontoon party boat! I got to meet another O'Keefe daughter, Colleen, and her husband Paul. Paul arrived by boat! My kids had a great time swinging on a rope into the lake, and later Paul took us tubing in his boat. When I told Ed that he had found a little slice of heaven, he quickly replied that he had another slice in Florida...his winter home on the beach! Ed had made a good living as an insurance salesman and was reaping the rewards in his retirement. I grilled Ed some more about his past. He served in the U.S. Navy during World War II, enlisting in February, 1943 at the tender age of 17. He received his training aboard a World War I battleship, the *Wyoming,* and was later assigned to a yard mine sweeper, the *YMS 104*, making the rank of quartermaster 3rd class. Ed told me,

"The crew was sea sick most of the time and could not stand the sight of food, but not me. I ate like King Kong!" I couldn't help but think it was strange that the son of a *Titanic* survivor would have such a connection to the water. First Ed became a sailor, then later in life he bought a house on a lake and another on the ocean!

I wrote to Lily Roche to tell her all about my visits with the O'Keefe's, but I didn't receive a reply for a long time. I later learned that Lily had suffered a heart attack. Heart problems still run in the family, but fortunately Lily survived and recovered fully.

Back at home, I did some more research to see what else I could find. I tried to get a copy of Pat and Anna's marriage license for myself and Ed, since he didn't have a copy. (It was probably in that steamer trunk!) When I applied for a copy, I found that New York City had no record of their marriage. We assumed they were married at City Hall or a local church in Manhattan where they lived, but it turns out they were married October 13, 1923 in Jersey City, New Jersey. Why they got married in New Jersey is a mystery, but I discovered this information when my cousin Patty Girl's husband Don sent me a copy of Pat's petition for naturalization. My grandfather Jack and his brother, Great Uncle Mickey, signed the petition as witnesses. I also visited the public library in the city of Newburgh, near where I lived, because they had microfilm copies of the *New York Times* going back a hundred years. Someone online had mentioned that Pat was interviewed by the *Times* along with many other survivors, so I started the tedious process of going through every copy of the paper from the first report of the sinking. It wasn't until the May 4th, 1912 edition that I finally found the mention of Pat:

"Patrick O'Keefe, an Irishman who sailed on the *Titanic* as a steerage passenger, after asking aid of the White Star yesterday and being referred to the Red Cross Society and the Irish Immigrant Home, told his experience. He believes he was one of the last to be saved. He swam toward a life raft when the steamship went down, and was hauled aboard. The raft was covered with firemen and other members of the crew. The raft had as many as it could hold when O'Keefe was dragged aboard, and of the scores struggling and fighting around them, not another man could scramble up to safety."

So, was Pat the last to climb aboard the overturned lifeboat, or the first, as reported in the Catholic newspaper? We'll never know for sure. Junior Wireless Operator Harold Bride later testified at the disaster hearings that he was the last man to be hauled aboard *Collapsible B*.

Well, I think it's time to sum up what I have learned, but as for what happened to Pat while he was still aboard *Titanic*, I will have to make some educated guesses.

34

UNITED STATES DISTRICT COURT
SOUTHERN DISTRICT OF NEW YORK.

IN THE MATTER

-of-

The Petition of the OCEANIC STEAM NAVIGATION COMPANY, LIMITED, owner of the steamship TITANIC for limitation of liability.

CLAIM OF PATRICK O'KEEFE

HARRINGTON, BIGHAM & ENGLAR
Proctors for Claimant,
64 WALL STREET, NEW YORK CITY

Pat's claim for damages from the Titanic disaster, still on file at the National Archives in New York.

Chapter Nine: The Pat O'Keefe Story

Patrick O'Keefe was born July 11, 1890 in Waterford, Ireland, the first of eight children to be born to John and Catherine O'Keefe of Little Michael Street. Besides Pat, the O'Keefe children included Jimmy, Johnny, Ellen, Susan, Mollie, Arthur and Eddie. Pat's father worked his way up from common laborer to become manager of a newspaper distributor. Pat's mother, the former Catherine Fitzgerald, died of liver disease in 1909 at the age of 37, leaving behind some very young children. Pat received a typical Catholic school education, first at the Sisters of Charity School for Boys and Girls, then with the Christian Brothers at De-La-Salle School, both in Waterford. Pat loved to swim, and would take his little brother Arthur for a dip in the chilly Suir River, even on Christmas Day. This did not please his father, who worried about the strong current there. When Patrick was a young man, he was employed as a porter and also helped on his father's trucks, dropping off the bundles of newspapers to dealers, but his father thought his son could do better for himself and encouraged him to find his fortune in America. At the age of 19, Pat decided to make the move. Before he left Ireland, his father commissioned a professional photographer to take a family portrait. Sadly, his mother died not long after the portrait was taken. Pat joined Uncles Arthur and Patrick "Patsy" O'Keefe and sailed to America in 1910 aboard the *S.S. Celtic*, departing Queenstown, Ireland on August 28th and arriving in New York on September 4th. Pat came over as a "non-immigrant alien" to work as a laborer. He stayed with his uncles at an apartment at 465 10th Avenue on the West Side of Manhattan, a tough neighborhood known as "Hell's Kitchen." He later moved in with a cousin, John Phelan, who lived nearby at 460 West 38th Street. After working hard and saving his money, Pat returned to Ireland in 1912 to spend a holiday with his family. His father had remarried by this time, to a woman named Johanna Brown, and they lived at Number Two Spring Garden Alley in Waterford City. Pat was scheduled to return to New York on the *Baltic*, but he was persuaded by his brother James to wait another week and spend Easter with the family in Ireland. Pat switched his passage to the *Titanic* for its maiden voyage. He was the only passenger from Waterford. His third class ticket, number 368402, cost him 7.15 pounds, or about $35.50 in American money. Pat headed to Queenstown, arriving on April 10th, the day before *Titanic* was due there. After checking into a hotel, he wired his father, admitting he felt "downhearted" about leaving Ireland again. That night Pat had a nightmare, in which he saw *Titanic* going down in the middle of the ocean. He thought of selling his ticket the next day, but didn't want to go back to Waterford and have all his friends laughing at him. Pat swallowed his bad feelings and boarded the tender that would take him out to where *Titanic*...and a place in history...were waiting.

Being a steerage passenger, Pat was housed in a cabin on one of the lower decks, very likely in the bow section where most single men were bunked in groups, and so he was probably immediately aware of the impact when *Titanic* struck the iceberg shortly before midnight, Sunday, April 14th. When Pat went on top to see what was the matter, he was assured by a steward that it was nothing serious and he was advised to return to his cabin. Meanwhile, the lifeboats were being uncovered and first class passengers were quietly being told to put on their lifebelts and go to the boat deck. When Pat returned to his cabin, he learned about the water coming into the ship, and he went back up. The lifeboats were being filled and Pat was now told to go back to his cabin and get his lifebelt. When he tried to do that, he found his cabin was filling up with water. With no lifebelt, he went up to the third class general room or smoking room, located on C deck at the stern, and watched the last of the lifeboats row away. He met two other third class passengers, Victor Sunderland and Edward Dorking, both from England, and they decided to jump from the steerage deck as the ocean washed over the forward end of the ship and the stern began to rise.

Pat swam away from the ship's side and came upon a "raft," as he called it. It turned out to be the overturned lifeboat, *Collapsible B*. The boat had flipped over as crew members hurriedly tried to launch it from the rapidly sinking ship. Some crew members had managed to climb onto it as it floated off the ship, but they were knocked off when the forward funnel collapsed and smacked the water, sending the overturned boat away from the ship. After climbing onto it, Pat pulled two other men on board, and the three of them paddled around, picking up others, including Sunderland and Dorking. They were also joined by Second Officer Charles Lightoller, first class passengers John "Jack" Thayer, Jr. and American Army Colonel Archibald Gracie, Chief Baker Charles Joughin and scullion John Collins, and Second Wireless Officer Harold Bride, who was trapped under the collapsible for a time. There were as many as 30 men on the overturned boat, but several died during the night. It is believed that First Wireless Officer Jack Phillips was one of the dead. When it became clear that taking on any additional swimmers would sink the overturned boat, the men of *Collapsible B* were forced to make the life and death decision of turning others away and paddling from the scene.

Once they were away, someone on the upturned boat suggested that they pray. Each man called out his religion, and they agreed to say the Lord's Prayer. Officer Lightoller then organized the men in standing positions to keep the boat balanced, and in the morning light, he could see the other lifeboats and signaled with his whistle. The men of *Collapsible B* were taken off by lifeboats number 4 and number 12. In the meantime, the rescue ship *Carpathia* had arrived, but it was another two hours before they were all aboard. Father Michael Kenny, a New York Catholic priest who visited survivors at St. Vincent's Hospital, was told that Pat O'Keefe was a hero and helped pull people onto the overturned boat. Father Kenny was also told that several women made it to the collapsible, but no ladies were rescued from the overturned boat when morning came. If women did make it to the boat, they did not last the night after being in the freezing water.

After being released from St. Vincent's Hospital, Pat returned to the apartment he shared with his cousin. He filed a claim against the

White Star line for his losses and injuries. Represented by the Wall Street firm of Harrington, Bigham and Englar, Pat claimed he lost baggage and valuables worth 250 dollars, and he asked for 10,000 dollars for his injuries from exposure and lost wages. Incredibly, he was offered only free passage on one of White Star's other ships back to Queenstown, if he would promise not to file suit in England. He decided to stay in America. Pat landed a new job for 12 dollars a week, decent pay in those days, and wrote a batch of letters to his father and friends back in Ireland to let them know he was alright. In those letters Pat revealed that he did not panic, and that a "cool head" saved him. He never returned to Ireland. His brothers Eddie and Arthur would later join him in America, and his sister Mollie (Margaret) may have immigrated as well, but Pat never saw his father or other siblings again.

Father Kenny wrote an article about Pat's heroism in the *Titanic* disaster, and it was published in a Catholic newspaper and was also printed in the Brooklyn, N.Y. *Daily Eagle*. Another account in the *New York Times* reported that Pat was the last or one of the last to be pulled aboard the overturned lifeboat. Other articles about him appeared in Ireland and England, but while other survivors wrote books and gave lectures, Pat chose to keep a low profile, and tried to forget the experience. He knew only too well the fate of those turned away from the overturned lifeboat on that dreadful night.

When World War One broke out, Pat was still a British subject and opted for military duty in Canada, as he refused to cross the ocean again, and surely had no love for the English army so soon after the nationalist uprising known as the "Easter Rebellion" was crushed back in Ireland. After the war, Pat returned to New York's West Side and met Jack Nolan and his younger sister, Anna. Although Anna was fifteen years younger, she and Pat fell in love and they were married on October 13, 1923 in Jersey City, New Jersey. The marriage produced two children, Margaret and Edward. Back in Ireland, Pat's brother John was killed in an ambush during the civil war that resulted when Ireland was divided into the Irish Free State and Northern Ireland.

Pat secured a job as an elevator operator at Number Two Rector Street, a large downtown office building. He was later promoted to elevator "starter," a supervisory position he held until his death. The O'Keefe's moved uptown to a nicer neighborhood, first to 973 Columbus Avenue, then to 120 West 109th Street. He kept up his friendship with Anna's brother Jack, and visited him often, always bringing the children along to play with Jack's kids, Tommy, Billy, Eddie and baby Anna, named after Pat's wife.

1939 was a tumultuous year for the O'Keefe family. Back in Ireland, Pat's father died of heart problems in June of that year. A month later, Pat finally became a U.S. citizen. The World's Fair came to New York that year, and Pat saved up money to take the family. On December 16, 1939, Pat accompanied his wife on a shopping trip. Anna went into a meat market and Pat waited outside to have a smoke. While Anna did her shopping, Pat collapsed in the street and died of a massive heart attack at the age of 49. He was pronounced dead on arrival at St. Luke's Hospital. A wake was held for him in his home, and he was buried December 19th at Gate of Heaven Cemetery in Hawthorne, New York. There is no mention of *Titanic* at his grave. In the spring of 1940, Anna fulfilled Pat's wish and took the children to the World's Fair.

Anna married again years later, to a man named Andy Bartlett. She died of heart failure in 1968 following a brief illness. She was 63. Daughter Margaret became an executive with Revlon Cosmetics. She never married and passed away in 1988 at the age of 64, as a result of complications from surgery to treat Crohn's Disease, an intestinal disorder. Anna and

Margaret were buried with Pat. After serving in the Navy during World War II, Edward became an insurance salesman and married Patricia Huson in 1948. They have four daughters, Patricia (nicknamed "Peachy"), Colleen, Margie and Jackie. Ed and Pat celebrated their 50th wedding anniversary in August of 1998, and today they divide their time between their home in upstate New York and their condo in Florida.

As it looks today, Pier 54 in New York, where the *Carpathia* brought *Titanic* survivors. The original steel girder frame of the entrance still stands and the dock has been restored. It is now part of New York City's Hudson River Park. Music and food festivals are held there in the summer.

St. Vincent's Hospital in New York, where *Titanic* survivors like Pat O'Keefe were treated for their injuries. It closed in 2010 due to financial problems.

Chapter Ten: The Men of Collapsible B

Who else was on the overturned lifeboat, *Collapsible B*, with Pat O'Keefe? I have already mentioned Second Officer Charles Lightoller, Junior Wireless Operator Harold Bride, Chief Baker Charles Joughin, Assistant Cook John Collins, first class passengers Archibald Gracie and John Thayer, and third class passengers Edward Dorking and Victor Sunderland. It is believed that a total of 28 survivors spent the night on the upturned boat. The most complete list I have seen is one compiled by Peter Engberg-Klarstrom and Chris Dohany, who came up with 27 names, including two who died on the boat.

It is believed that Jack Phillips, the Senior Wireless Operator, made it to the collapsible but slipped off and died during the night. Third class passenger Abraham Harmer died on the collapsible. Besides Gracie and Thayer, one other first class passenger was aboard: Algernon Barkworth. Only one second class passenger made it to the boat: William Mellors. In addition to the third class passengers already mentioned, there was Albert Moss. The rest of the men who swam to the overturned boat were crew members such as firemen, stokers, trimmers and greasers, stewards and cooks. Firemen tended the fires in the ship's furnaces, stokers shoveled the coal into the furnace, trimmers broke up large chunks of coal in the coal bunker and brought the coal in wheelbarrows to the stokers, and greasers applied grease to the moving parts of the ship's engines. Stewards set tables and waited on passengers, and cooks...well, of course, they cooked the food. The other *Collapsible B* survivors included firemen Harry Senior and Charles Judd, and trimmers A. Hebb, James McGann, John O'Connor, Ernest Allen, and Eustace Snow. Also saved were greasers Walter Hurst and George Pregnall, and mess steward Charles Fitzpatrick. Saloon steward Thomas Whitely was there, along with third class steward Sidney Daniels and entree cook John Maynard.

In his account of the disaster, Colonel Gracie mentioned two others on the upset boat, crew member J. Hagan and Seaman J. McGough, but Gracie was not certain about McGough, who, it turns out, was actually assigned to lifeboat number 9 and was rescued from there.

And what about Captain Smith himself? Fireman Harry Senior and entree cook John Maynard said they saw Captain Smith clinging to the boat, but that he was unable to keep his hold and slipped off.

To get a feel for what it was like on the overturned boat I read several books containing eyewitness accounts. I first picked up a paperback edition of <u>The Titanic Disaster Hearings: The Official Transcripts of the 1912 Senate Investigation,</u> edited by Tom Kuntz of the "New York Times," published by Pocket Books. The hearings were held by a subcommittee of the Committee on Commerce of the United States Senate, chaired by Senator William Alden Smith, a Republican from Michigan. The hearings began Friday, April 19, 1912 at the Waldorf-Astoria Hotel in New York City, just one day after the *Carpathia* arrived with survivors at Pier 54 in New York. With the tragedy still fresh in the minds of survivors, the transcripts of testimony provide an amazing look at the disaster before the passage of time and media influence could have an effect on survivor accounts. Pat O'Keefe was not called to testify, and of the 88 witnesses who did testify in person or in writing, only four were survivors from *Collapsible B*. They were Second Officer Lightoller, Wireless Operator Bride, assistant cook John Collins and Colonel Gracie.

   I pored over their testimony in search of any reference to Pat. They assumed most of those aboard the overturned boat were crew members. Lightoller was the first of the four to testify:

Senator Smith: Do you know any of the men

who were in the water as you were and who boarded this lifeboat?

Mr. Lightoller: Yes, sir.

Senator Smith: Give their names.

Mr. Lightoller: Mr. Thayer, a first class passenger; the second Marconi operator--I can tell you his name in a minute--Bride.

Senator Smith: Was that the boat that Col. Gracie---

Mr. Lightoller: Oh, yes; and Col. Gracie.

Senator Smith: Was he on the upturned boat before you got it righted around?

Mr. Lightoller: We never righted it.

Senator Smith: You never righted it?

Mr. Lightoller: No, sir; we could not.

Senator Smith: Who else was there?

Mr. Lightoller: I think all the rest were firemen taken out of the water, sir. Those are the only passengers that I know of.

Senator Smith: No other passengers?

Mr. Lightoller: There were two or three that died. I think there were three or four who died during the night.

Senator Smith: Aboard this boat with you?

Mr. Lightoller: Yes, sir; I think the senior Marconi operator was on the boat and died. The Marconi junior operator told me that the senior was on this boat and died.

Senator Smith: From the cold?

Mr. Lightoller: Presumably.

Senator Smith: How many persons altogether?

Mr. Lightoller: I should roughly estimate about 30. She was packed standing from stem to stern at daylight.

Senator Smith: Was there any effort made by others to board her?

Mr. Lightoller: We took all on board that we could.

Junior wireless operator Bride was the next to testify:

Senator Smith: Do you know any of the people that were on that boat besides Mr. Phillips and yourself?

Mr. Bride: There was an officer, I believe, on the boat.

Senator Smith: An officer?

Mr. Bride: And there was a passenger; I could not see whether he was first, second or third.

Senator Smith: What kind of a looking man?

Mr. Bride: I could not say, sir.

Senator Smith: Have you learned who it was?

Mr. Bride: No, sir; I heard him say at the time he was a passenger.

Senator Smith: Was it Col. Gracie?

Mr. Bride: I could not say. He merely said he was a passenger.

Senator Smith: Where did he get on?

Mr. Bride: I could not say. I was the last man they invited on board.

Senator Smith: Were there others struggling to get on?

Mr. Bride: Yes, sir.

Senator Smith: How many?

Mr. Bride: Dozens.

Senator Smith: Dozens. In the water?

Mr. Bride: Yes, sir.

Senator Smith: With life preservers on?

Mr. Bride: Yes, sir.

Senator Smith: Was this one man the only passenger?

Mr. Bride: I could not say.

Senator Smith: Did anyone say to you that anyone else was a passenger?

Mr. Bride: No, sir; we did not have much to say to each other.

Senator Smith: You did not talk to one another?

Mr. Bride: No, sir.

Senator Smith: Do you know whether the other occupants of that boat were officers or seamen or stewards or employees?

Mr. Bride: I should judge they were all employees. They were all part of the boat's crews.

    The next *Collapsible B* survivor to testify was 17 year old John Collins of Belfast, Ireland, who was an assistant cook in *Titanic's* first class galley. He told committee member Senator Bourne the heart-rending tale of being washed from the deck, losing hold of a child he was carrying. Collins may have seen Pat O'Keefe on the overturned boat after it was washed clear by the collapse of the forward funnel. It's hard to tell from the way he speaks, as he jumps back and forth from the time the crew was trying to launch the collapsible to the time he came to the surface of the water.

Mr. Collins: ....When I came to the surface I saw this boat that had been taken off. I saw a man on it. They had been working on it, taking it off of the saloon deck, and when the waves washed it off the deck they clung to that; then I made for it when I came to the surface and saw it, and I swam over to it.

Senator Bourne: Did you have a life belt on?

Mr. Collins: I had, sir. I was only about 4 or 5 yards off of it, and I swam over to it and I got on to it.

Senator Bourne: How many were on the collapsible boat?

Mr. Collins: Well, sir, I could not exactly say; but I am sure there was more than 15 or 16.

Senator Bourne: Did those who were on help you get on?

Mr. Collins: No, sir; they were all watching the ship. I had not much to do. All I had to do was give a spring and I got onto it; and we were drifting about for two hours on the water.

The last of the *Collapsible B* survivors to testify at the American inquiry was American Army Colonel Archibald Gracie, an eloquent man who was already a published author before writing his account of the *Titanic* disaster. Colonel Gracie went down with the ship after helping to load the lifeboats.

Senator Smith: Was the water cold?

Mr. Gracie: I did not notice any coldness of the water at that time. I was too much preoccupied in getting away.

Senator Smith: Did it have any bad effect on you?

Mr. Gracie: No, not then, but afterwards, on the raft. I was on the raft, which I will speak of, all night; and I did not notice how cold the water was until I got on the raft. There was a sort of gulp, as if something had occurred, behind me, and I suppose that was where the water was closing up, where the ship had gone down; but the surface of the water was perfectly still; and there were, I say, this wreckage and these bodies, and there were the horrible sounds of drowning people and people gasping for breath. While collecting the wreckage together I got on a big wooden crate, some sort of a wooden crate, or wood of that sort. I saw an upturned boat, and I struck out for that boat, and there I saw what I supposed were members of the crew on this upset boat. I grabbed the arm of one of them and pulled myself up on this boat.

Senator Smith: Did anybody resist you at all?

Mr. Gracie: What is that?

Senator Smith: Was there any resistance offered?

Mr. Gracie: Oh, no; none whatever. I was among the first. I suppose the boat was then about half full.

Senator Smith: How many were on it?

Mr. Gracie: I suppose there must have been between 15 and 20.

Senator Smith: Was Officer Lightoller on it?

Mr. Gracie: Yes, Officer Lightoller was on that same boat.

Senator Smith: At that time?

Mr. Gracie: At that same time. Then I came up to the surface and was told by Lightoller what had occurred. One of the funnels fell from the steamer, and was falling toward him, but when it was going to strike him, young Mr. Thayer, who was also on the same boat, said that it splashed near him, within 15 yards, he said, and it splashed him toward this raft. We climbed on this raft. There was one man who was in front, with an oar, and another man in the stern with what I think was a piece of a board, propelling the boat along. Then we loaded the raft, as we now call it, with as many as it would contain, until she became under water, until we could take no more, because the water was up to our waists.

I remembered that Dr. Andy Bielenberg of Ireland suggested that I read Colonel Gracie's book about the *Titanic* disaster. It was first published posthumously in 1913 as The Truth About The Titanic, but has been re-issued as Titanic: A Survivor's Story. The Colonel devotes an entire chapter to his night on the upturned boat, which he referred to as "the Engelhardt," since the collapsible type boat was named after its builder, Captain Engelhardt of Copenhagen, Denmark. I couldn't find a copy of the book in any of the local libraries, but luckily I was able to purchase a new edition put out by Academy Chicago Publishers which includes *The Sinking of the S.S .Titanic* by John B. Thayer, or "young Jack Thayer" as he was known on Titanic. I got two *Collapsible B* survivor accounts for the price of one!

When Colonel Gracie first climbed aboard the Engelhardt he was uncomfortable with the company he was keeping and was offended by the language used by some of the other men, who referred to the less fortunate victims as "the blokes swimming in the water." He may have heard Pat O'Keefe speak, since my father told me that Pat always called guys "blokes." Gracie later realized it was just their way of speaking and they weren't being unsympathetic toward those who couldn't make it to the boat. I had heard a story that Colonel Gracie got into a mild argument with someone on the overturned boat when he asked to borrow a cap to warm his head. After seeing the family portrait of Pat with his cap and hearing from family members who said Pat always wore a hat, I had to find out if Pat was the one. Colonel Gracie believed some of the men who still had their caps were able to swim from *Titanic's* side without getting sucked under and getting their heads wet as he did. When he asked one of the men for the loan of his cap for a short while, the man's response was "And what wad oi do?" The man spoke with a cockney accent, not an Irish accent, so it couldn't have been Pat. Pat probably lost his cap when he leaped from the steerage deck. Based on what I have learned of Pat's generosity, I believe that if he had a dry cap at the time, he would have given it to Colonel Gracie.

The Colonel's book also contains testimony and quotes from other *Collapsible B* survivors who were not allowed on at first. Gracie quotes Chief Baker Joughin from his testimony in the British inquiry: "I got on to the starboard side of the poop; found myself in the water. I do not believe my head went under the water at all. I thought I saw some wreckage. Swam towards it and found collapsible boat ("B") with Lightoller and about twenty-five men on it. There was no room for me. I tried to get on, but was pushed off, but I hung around. I got around to the opposite side and cook Maynard, who recognized me, helped me and held on to me."

Gracie also quotes Steward Thomas Whiteley from his interview in the *New York Tribune:* "I drifted near a boat wrong-side-up. About 30 men were clinging to it. They refused to let me get on. Somebody tried to hit me with an oar, but I scrambled on to her." Fireman Harry Senior is quoted from the *London Illustrated News* and *New York Times*: "I tried to get aboard of her, but some chap hit me over the head with an oar. There were too many on her. I got around to the other side of the boat and climbed on. There were thirty-five of us, including the second officer, and no women. I saw any amount of drowning and dead around us."

Did Great Uncle Pat whack anybody to keep the boat from being swamped? We'll probably never know.

The Sinking of the S.S. Titanic by John Thayer, Jr. was published privately for family members in 1940. Only 17 at the time of the sinking, Thayer lost his father and was forever haunted by the experience. He was sucked down not once, but twice! Thayer and a companion, Milton Long, jumped from the starboard rail when the deck was only "twelve or fifteen feet above the water." Long perished and his body was later recovered. Young Thayer was sucked down, "spinning in all directions." When he came to the surface, he floated with the aid of his life preserver and watched *Titanic* go down. He said the ship appeared to split in two, and he was sucked down again when the second funnel fell near him:

"It looked as if it would fall on top of me. It missed me by only twenty or thirty feet. The suction of it drew me down and down, struggling and swimming, practically spent. As I finally came to the surface I put my hand over my head, in order to push away any obstruction. My hand came against something smooth and firm with rounded shape. I looked up, and realized that it was the cork fender of one of the collapsible lifeboats, which was floating in the water bottom side up. About four or five men were clinging to her bottom. I pulled myself up as far as I could, almost exhausted, but I could not get my legs up. I asked them to give me a hand up, which they readily did."

Fortunately for Thayer, he was among the first to reach the upturned boat. Colonel Gracie was still struggling under water during *Titanic's* final plunge but Thayer and surely Pat O'Keefe watched from the "raft." Thayer described Titanic's last moments and the horror that followed:

"Her deck was turned slightly toward us. We could see groups of the almost fifteen hundred people still aboard, clinging in clusters or bunches, like swarming bees; only to fall in masses, pairs or singly, as the great after part of the ship, two hundred and fifty feet of it, rose into the sky, til it reached a sixty-five or seventy degree angle. Here it seemed to pause, and just hung, for what felt like minutes. Gradually she turned her deck away from us, as though to hide from our sight the awful spectacle.

We had an oar on our overturned boat. In spite of several men working it, amid our cries and prayers, we were being gradually sucked in toward the great pivoting mass. I looked upwards--we were right underneath the three enormous propellers. For an instant, I thought they were sure to come right down on top of us. Then, with the deadened noise of the bursting of her last few gallant bulkheads, she slid quietly away from us into the sea.

There was no final apparent suction, and practically no wreckage that we could see. I don't remember all the wild talk and calls that were going on on our boat, but there was one concerted sigh or sob as she went from view.

Probably a minute passed with almost dead silence and quiet. Then an individual call for help, from here, from there; gradually swelling into a composite volume of one long continuous wailing chant, from the fifteen hundred in the water all around us. It sounded like locusts on a mid-summer night, in the woods in Pennsylvania.

This terrible continuing cry lasted for twenty or thirty minutes, gradually dying away, as one after another could no longer withstand the cold and exposure. Practically no one was drowned, as no water was found in the lungs of those later recovered. Everyone had on a life preserver.

The partially filled lifeboats standing by, only a few hundred yards away, never came back. Why on earth they did not come back is a mystery. How could any human being fail to heed those cries?"

Those cries stayed with Jack Thayer and every other survivor until the day they died. It is no wonder that Pat O'Keefe never spoke of *Titanic*, and didn't even tell his own son about that night. Perhaps he was waiting until Ed was older. He was waiting for the right time to tell him. It never came.

"We have loved him during life; let us not abandon him, until we have conducted him by our prayers into the house of the Lord."
ST. AMBROSE

IN YOUR CHARITY
Pray for the Repose of the soul of

Patrick O'Keefe
+++ Who Died +++
On Dec. 16th, 1939

PRAYER

Gentlest Heart of Jesus, ever present in the Blessed Sacrament, ever consumed with burning love for the poor captive souls in Purgatory, have mercy on the soul of Thy servant, bring him far from the shadow of exile to the bright home of Heaven, where, we trust, Thou and Thy Blessed Mother, have woven for him a crown of unending bliss. Amen.

May He Rest in Peace. Amen.

Your gentle face and patient smile
   With sadness we recall.
You had a kindly word for each
   And died beloved by all.

The voice is mute and stilled the heart
   That loved us well and true,
Ah, bitter was the trial to part
   From one so good as you.

You are not forgotten loved one
   Nor will you ever be
As long as life and memory last
   We will remember thee.

We miss you now, our hearts are sore,
   As time goes by we miss you more,
Your loving smile, your gentle face
   No one can fill your vacant place.

Chapter Eleven: The Fate of Others

Pat O'Keefe was not the only *Titanic* survivor who still ironically met an untimely end or otherwise tragic death. Robert Douglas Spedden was a little boy when he was rescued from the *Titanic* sinking in 1912. One of the most published photos of *Titanic* shows Robert spinning a top on the promenade deck. The photo also survived because it was taken by Father Francis Browne, who traveled only the first leg of *Titanic's* maiden voyage from Southhampton to Queenstown. Three years after the sinking, nine year old Robert was killed in a car accident in Maine. His father, Frederick Spedden, another *Titanic* survivor, lived to be an old man, but suffered a heart attack in a swimming pool in Florida and drowned in 1947! That a *Titanic* survivor would later meet death beneath the surface of the water is indeed a cruel twist of fate.

Titanic lookout Frederick Fleet, the man who spotted the iceberg, was among those saved and, although he lived to be 77 years of age, he did not die a natural death. In a fit of despair related to financial problems and the death of his elderly wife, he hanged himself in 1965.

Colonel Gracie, who survived the same way as Pat O'Keefe, by swimming through 28 degree water to the overturned collapsible lifeboat, died just eight months after the disaster. Gracie was very active to the end. He testified at the hearings, contacted many other survivors, and wrote a book about the experience, but his body was 54 years old, not 21 like Pat O'Keefe's, and he never fully recovered from the ordeal. In December of 1912 he succumbed to pleurisy, a disease affecting the membrane that envelops the lungs.

Jack Thayer, another *Collapsible B* survivor, lost his father on *Titanic*, but tried to live a normal life. It was Thayer who saw *Titanic* break in two as it sank, but his claim was disputed during the hearings that followed the disaster. He later had a family of his own, but after losing one of his sons during World War Two, he took his own life in 1945 at the age of 50. Another great loss was too much for him. On a brighter note, I came across the name "Shine," while going through the list of survivors. My wife's sister Kathleen married a man named Frank Shine. Ellen Natalia Shine, a 20 year old third class passenger from County Cork, Ireland, made it to a lifeboat and survived. She stayed in New York after the disaster and lived on Long Island. She passed away in 1993 at the age of 101, the last remaining *Titanic* Survivor from Ireland. Is my brother-in-law also related to a Titanic survivor? Well, that's a research project for another day.

There were also people who survived the *Titanic* sinking who may have wished they had not. J. Bruce Ismay, managing director of the White Star line, was called a "rank coward," and roasted in the American press for getting into a lifeboat. A year later he was no longer director and lived out his life in near seclusion. 21 year old Irish immigrant Daniel Buckley, who was the same age as Pat O'Keefe, admitted at the hearings in New York that he cried when men were ordered out of the lifeboat he had jumped into. Buckley allowed a woman, apparently Mrs. Astor, to cover him with her shawl and he escaped detection. For the rest of his life, though, he faced accusations that he survived by dressing as a woman. Masabumi Hosono of Japan jumped into a lifeboat as it was being lowered. When he returned to his native country, he was branded a coward, fired from his job and forever shamed.

And so, by comparison to the fate of some of the others, Pat O'Keefe managed to make the most of his remaining years, and lived a good... albeit short... life. By all accounts, he was a modest man, generous, a good father and husband, a loyal worker, and trusted friend. Well, my search is over. I'm glad I found "Great

Uncle Pat." In doing so, I found my own roots as well, and I'm grateful to the many people who helped me along the way.

They say there was no moon the night *Titanic* sank. On chilly moonless nights I sometimes look up at the stars and think of my great uncle. I shiver as I wonder, "What if I had to jump into the middle of the ocean right now? What if I was faced with a situation where I knew I was going to die?" You can't think about *Titanic* without thinking about death. After finishing this book in 2000, I had a near-death experience of my own. I went to bed with severe back pain one evening and woke to find myself being loaded onto a stretcher by an ambulance crew. I had suffered a seizure, then developed pneumonia and, later, x-rays showed two fractures in my spine. My wife Mary is a nurse, and when she came to bed she realized I was seizing, not snoring as I have been known to do. I fully recovered, but the exact cause of it all was never determined. Doctors decided that it was probably epilepsy, since it runs in my family, but I had to wonder why it remained dormant for so long. While in the hospital I developed a new appreciation for life, and like Pat O'Keefe, I was glad to be alive.

CHAPTER TWELVE: PASSAGES

It is now 2012 and I have updated this book slightly for the 100th anniversary of the sinking of *Titanic*. I have left the original story largely intact to preserve the flow of events as they occurred. Since this book was first published in 2001, several key figures in this story have passed away, beginning with my father on August 1, 2010 at the age of 79. My father had been ill for some time and was living in a nursing home. He suffered from emphysema, Parkinson's disease and dementia. It was hard to watch this once strong man slowly wither away. I felt so helpless and even useless at times. Although I knew it was impossible, I wanted him to get well again. I wanted my father. I needed to talk to him. We were all with him when he breathed his last, and I just didn't want to let go. It was selfish of me, because I knew how much he had suffered from his illnesses and that his death would take away all pain and bring him peace.

I received a shock later that year when I learned Lily's son Sean passed away unexpectedly on November 20th at only 46 years of age, and that Lily was placed in a nursing home herself. I received this news from Sean's twin sister, Paula Walsh, whom I had not corresponded with previously. I was glad to get to know her a little, but it wasn't long before she had to tell me that Lily joined her son and passed away on January 21, 2011 at the age of 85.

    Ed O'Keefe is still alive at the time of this writing. The story of *Titanic* goes on forever.

Me and Dad in Hell's Kitchen, a very long time ago.

John Nolan

Made in the USA
Charleston, SC
21 April 2012